© All Rights Reserved

No part of this publication can be reproduced, stored in a retrieval system or transmitted, in any form or by any means, electronic, mechanical, photocopying, recording or otherwise without the prior permission of the Authors.

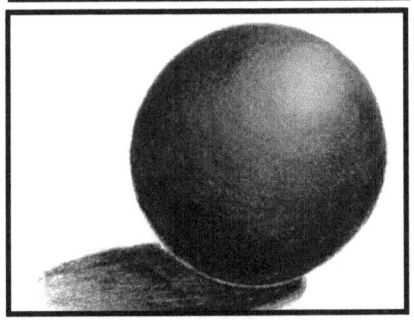

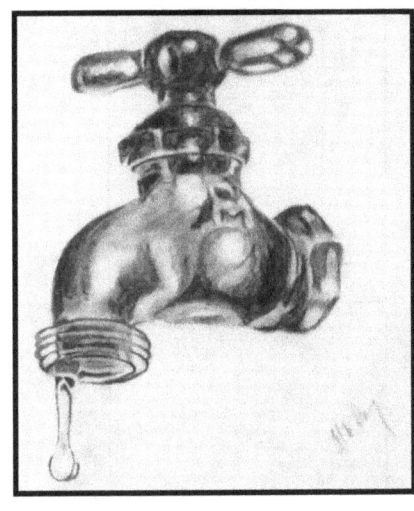

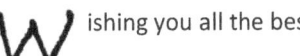

W ishing you all the best.

Welcome to Creative Canvas.

Student are say that whatever we see in social media, it is difficult to remember such videos. Not getting all the materials at once. That there should be a book in which all the material to be practiced together so that we can do this without any help.

That's why I have tried to give all the material together.

Just as we get excited or warm-Up in the beginning of sports or yoga. In music meditation also we all do warm up i.e. Swara Sadhna like - sa, re, ga, ma, pa, dha, ni, sa. Which can also be called basic fundamental practice. In this drawing book also some pictures of everyday practice have been series.

The box was made in this book design so that children's time is not wasted. This type of book design is happening for the first time. It is guaranteed that whoever practices it with meditation will get good results.

As a beginner, you should be able to hold your pencil in a way that encourages a smooth transition from the imagination of this drawing book.

Don't get tired of hands. To reach that level, you can practice with this book first. When you practice, you can read this book

Complete your lines and angles with the guidance of Soon you can take your drawing talent forward, you will be drawing on your own.

The content of this book has the undermentioned features. It has essential guidance to aspect of skill enhancement for learners and those who pursue it as Hobby.

Further suggestions for its improvement are welcomed.

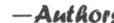
—Authors

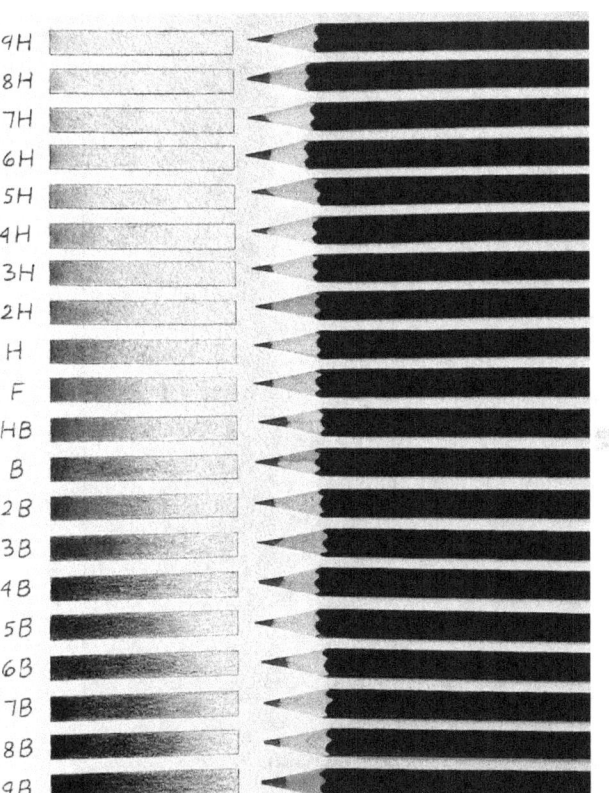

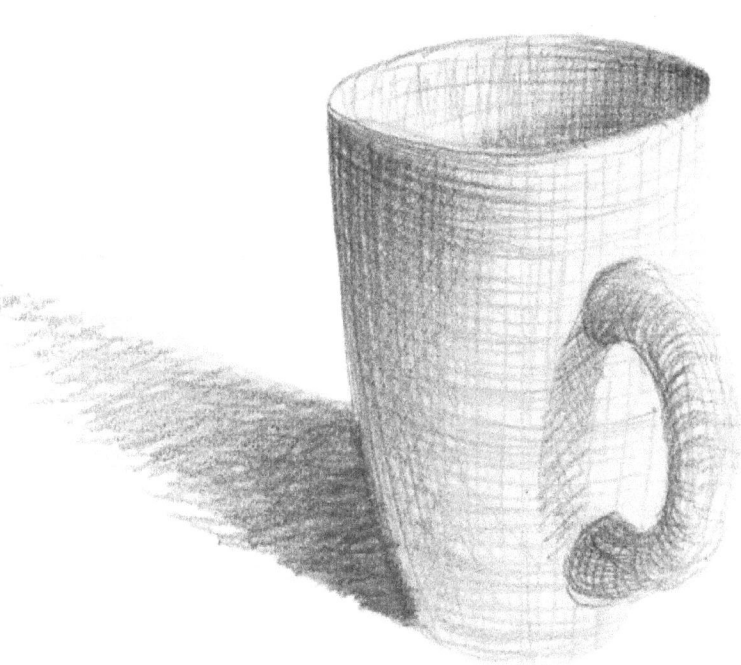

Draw straight line without help of ruler or any object (Use 4B or 6B Pencil)

Ex :- 1
Join the dots & diagonal line   (Move your pencil Left to Right up direction)

Pg-1

Draw straight line without help of ruler or any object (Use 4B or 6B Pencil)

Ex :- 2
Join the dots & diagonal line   ↙↙   (Move your pencil right top to left direction)

Pg-2

Draw straight line without help of ruler or any object (Use 4B or 6B Pencil)

Ex :- 3
Join the dots & diagonal line ↖↖ (Move your pencil from right bottom to left up direction)

Pg-3

Draw straight line without help of ruler or any object (Use 4B or 6B Pencil)

Ex :- 4
Join the dots & diagonal line   (Move your pencil from left up to right direction)

Pg-4

Draw straight line without help of ruler or any object (Use 4B or 6B Pencil)

Ex :- 5
Horizontal line

(Move your pencil left to right direction)

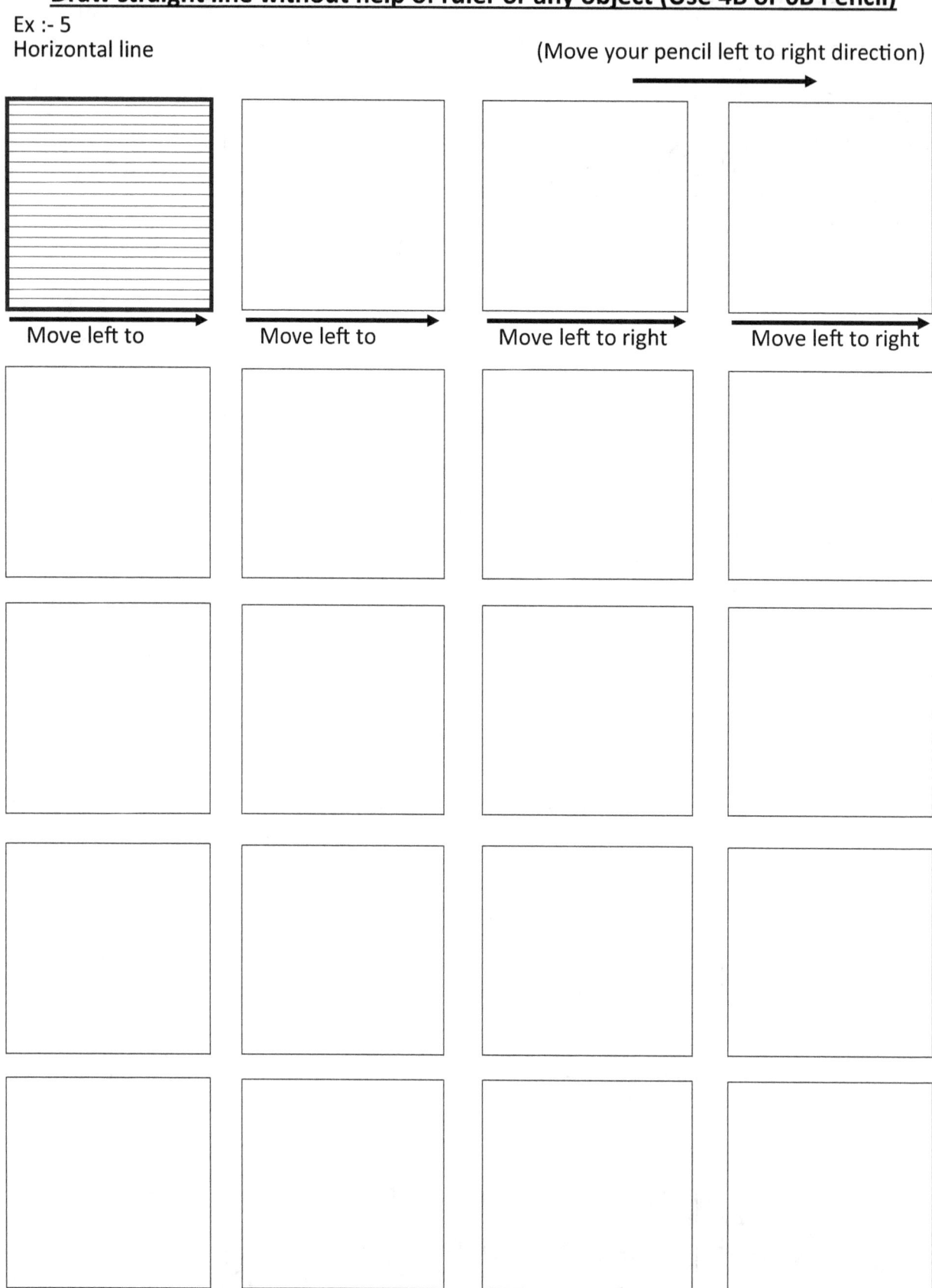

Move left to | Move left to | Move left to right | Move left to right

Pg-5

Draw straight line without help of ruler or any object (Use 4B or 6B Pencil)

Ex :- 6
Horizontal line   (Move your pencil right to left direction)

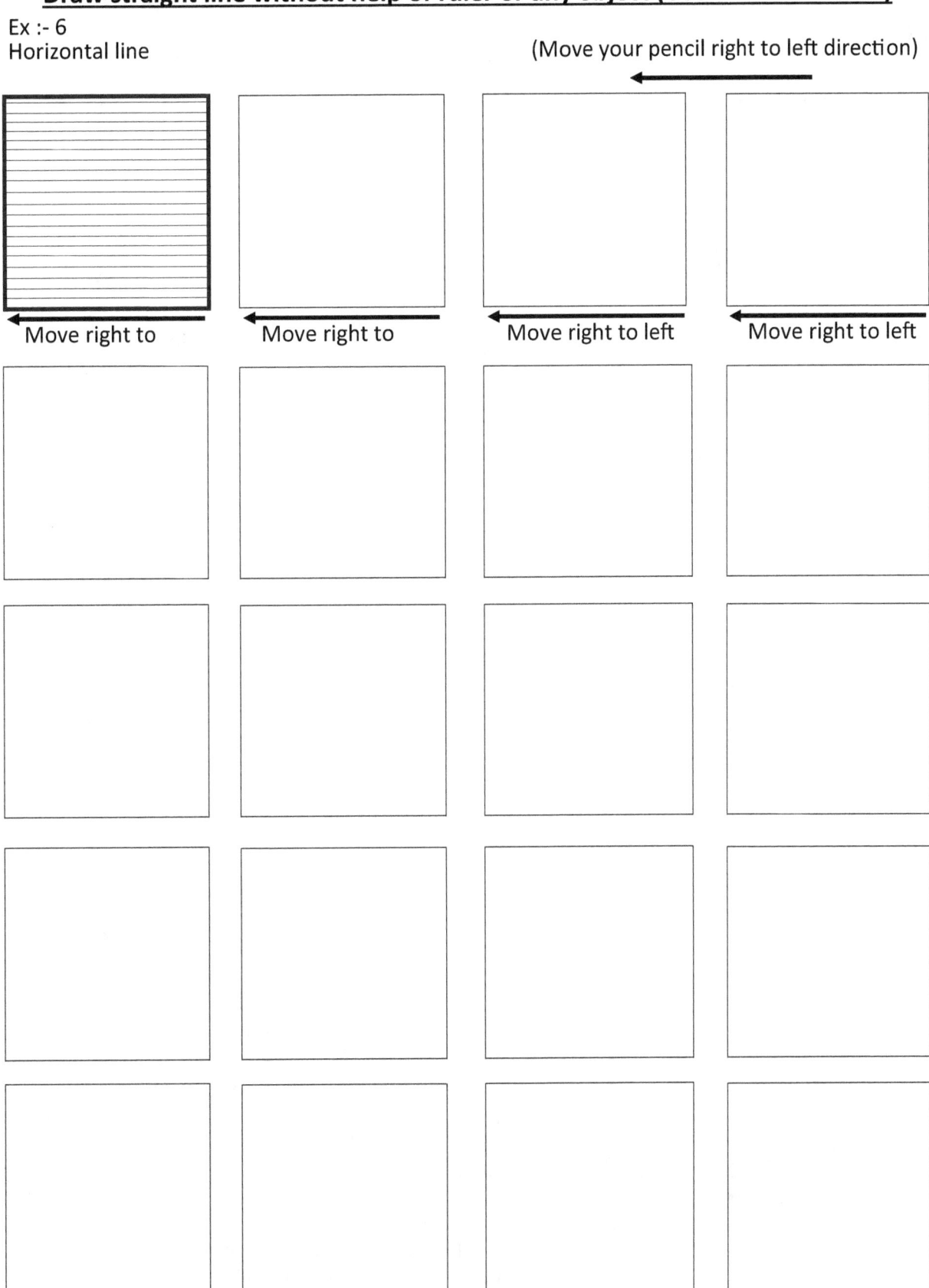

Pg-6

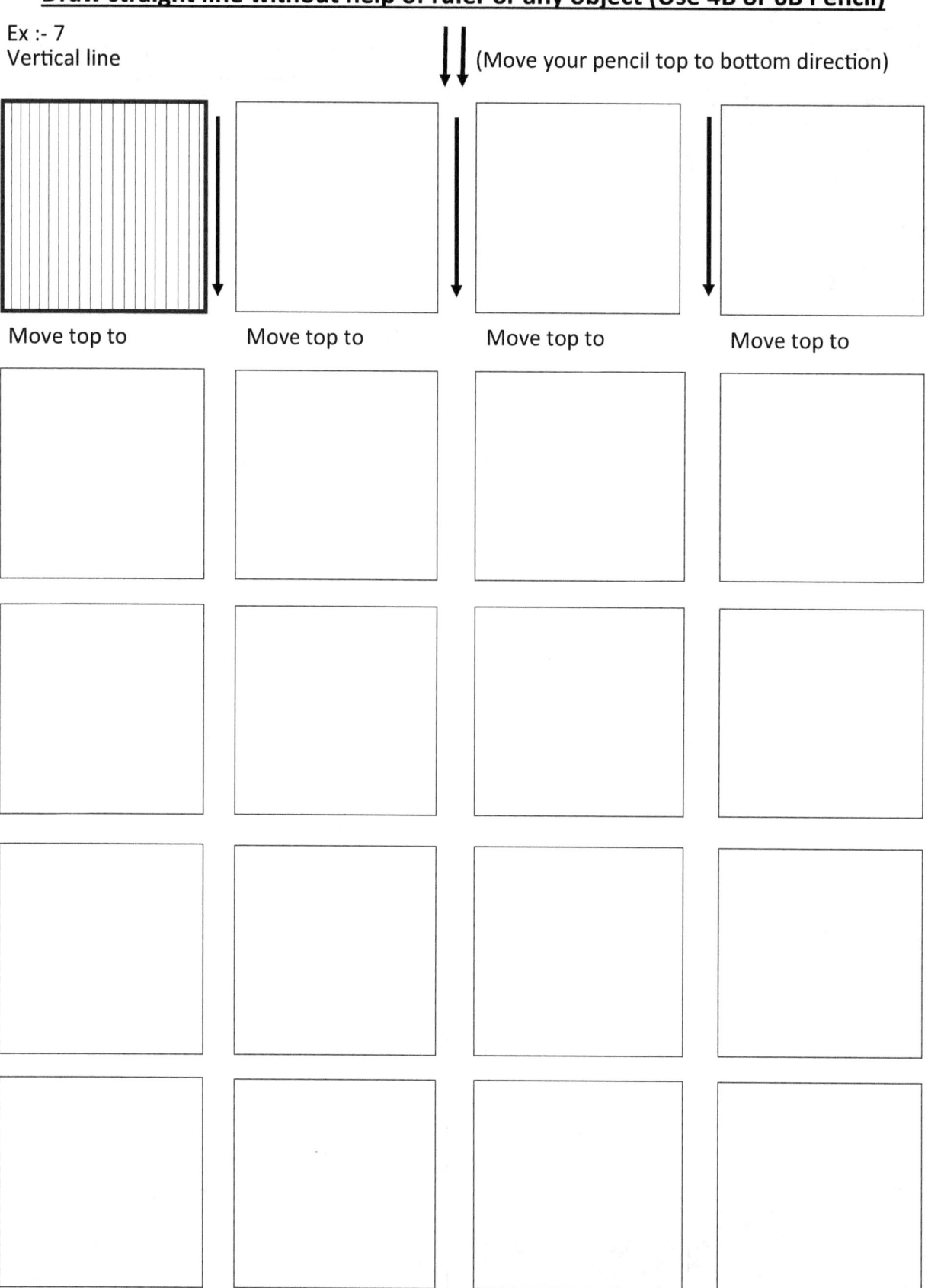

Draw straight line without help of ruler or any object (Use 4B or 6B Pencil)

Ex :- 8
Vertical line   (Move your pencil bottom to top direction)

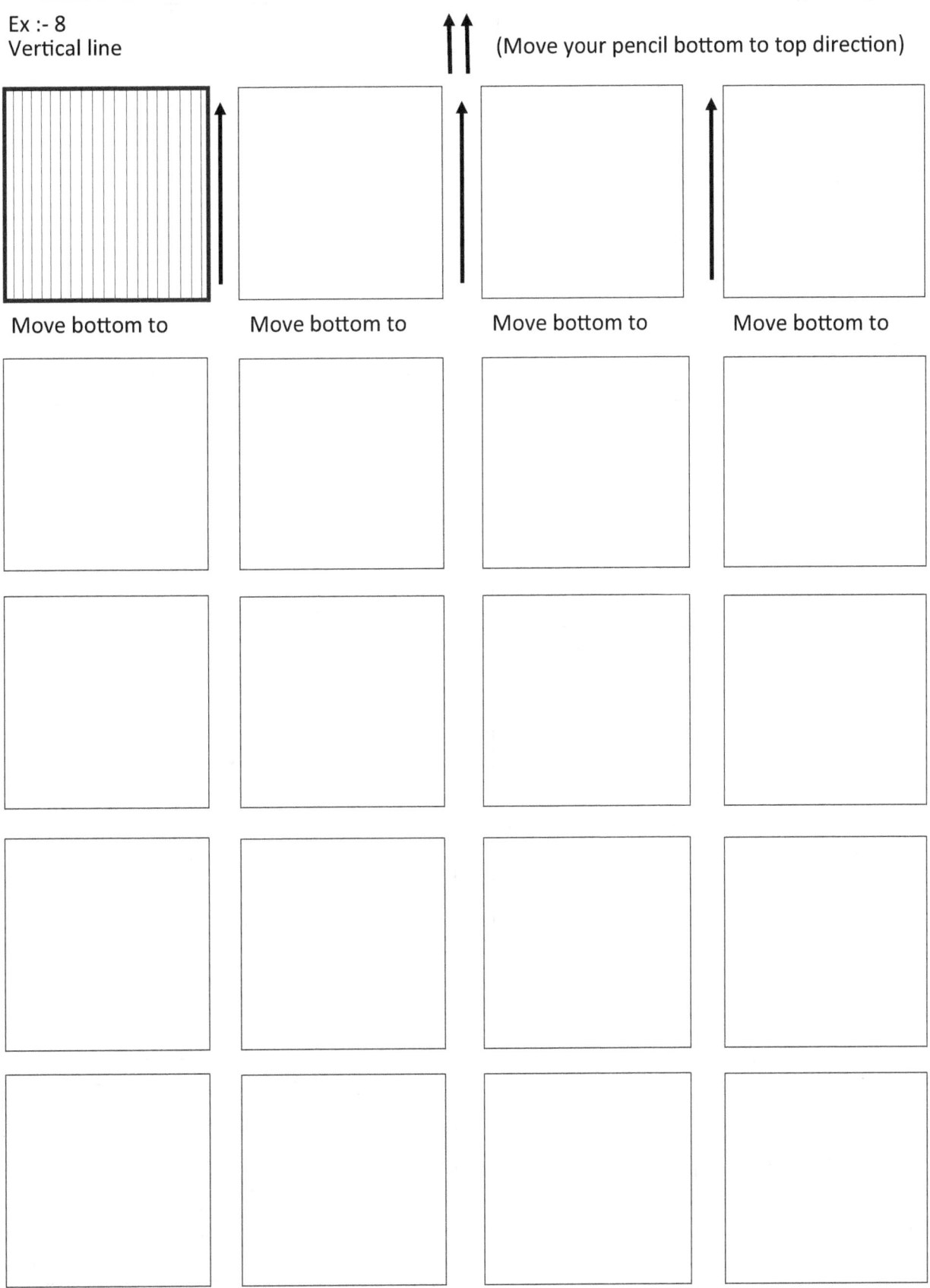

Move bottom to   Move bottom to   Move bottom to   Move bottom to

Draw curved line

Do **Don't** **(Use 4B or 6B Pencil)**

Ex :- 9
Draw curved line

(Move your pencil clock wise direction)

Move clock | Move clock | Move clock | Move clock

Pg-9

Draw curved line

Ex :- 10

Draw curved line

(Use 4B or 6B Pencil)

Move your pencil anti clock wise direction)

Draw curved line (Use 4B or 6B Pencil)

Ex :- 11
Draw curved line

(Move your pencil anti-clock wise direction)

Move anti- clock | Move anti- clock | Move anti- clock | Move anti- clock wise

Pg-11

Draw scribble   (Use 4B or 6B Pencil)

Ex :- 12

Draw scribble

Draw stripling   (Use 4B or 6B Pencil)

Ex :- 13
Draw stripling

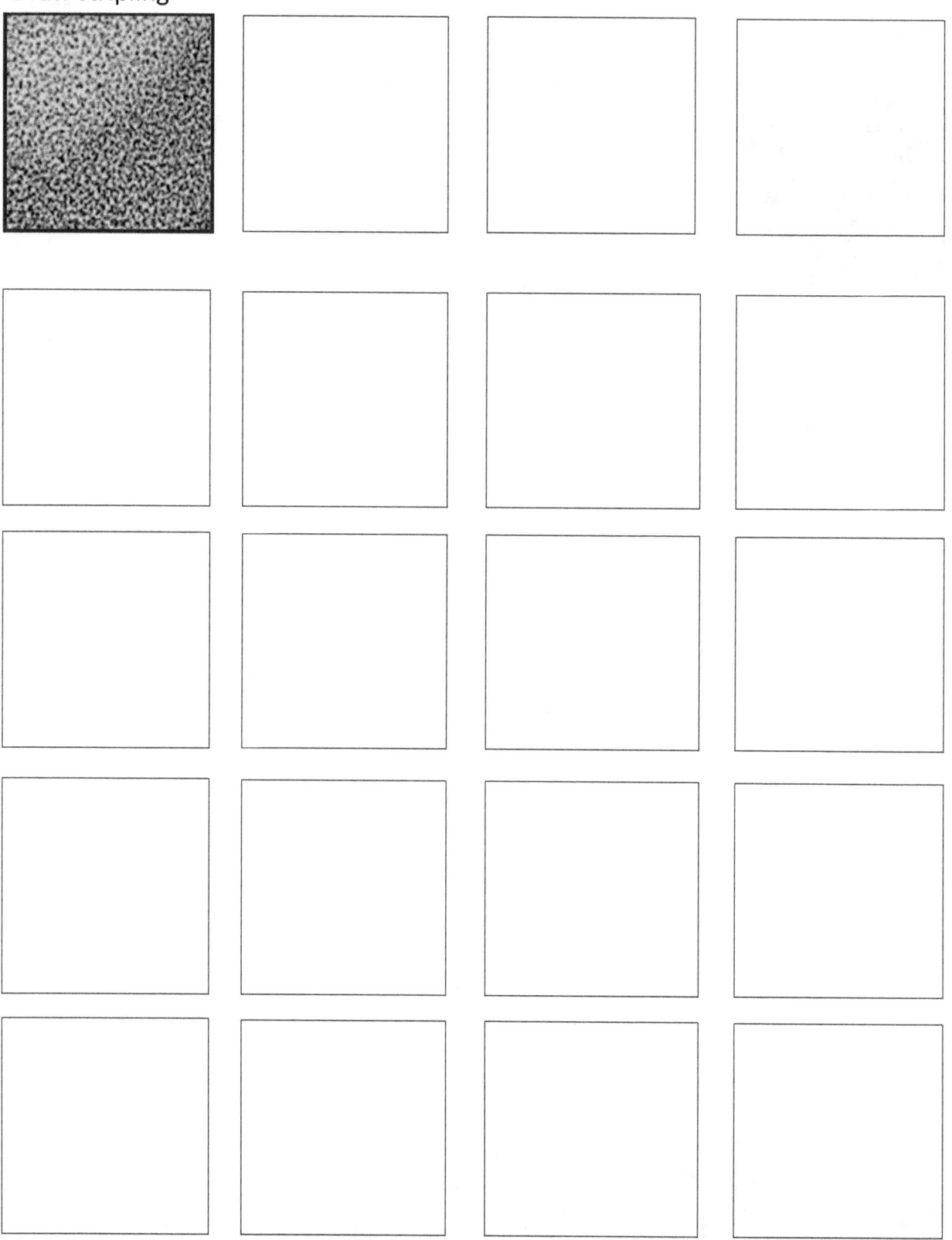

Draw broken line   (Use 4B or 6B Pencil)

Ex :- 14

Draw broken line   ⇔   (Move your pencil right to left direction)

Pg-14

Draw broken line

(Use 4B or 6B Pencil)

Ex :- 15

Draw broken line ⇒ (Move your pencil left to right direction)

Pg-15

Draw scribble (Use 4B or 6B Pencil)

Ex :- 16

Light to dark ⇒ (Move your pencil left to right direction)

Pg-16

Draw scribble ## (Use 4B or 6B Pencil)

Ex :- 17

Dark to light ⇒ (Move your pencil left to right direction)

Draw stripling (Use 4B or 6B Pencil)

Ex :- 18

Light to dark ⇒ (Move your pencil left to right direction)

Pg-18

Draw stripling   (Use 4B or 6B Pencil)

Ex :- 19

Dark to light   ⇒   (Move your pencil left to right direction)

Pg-19

Draw cross hatch

(Use 4B or 6B Pencil)

Ex :- 20

Cross hatch

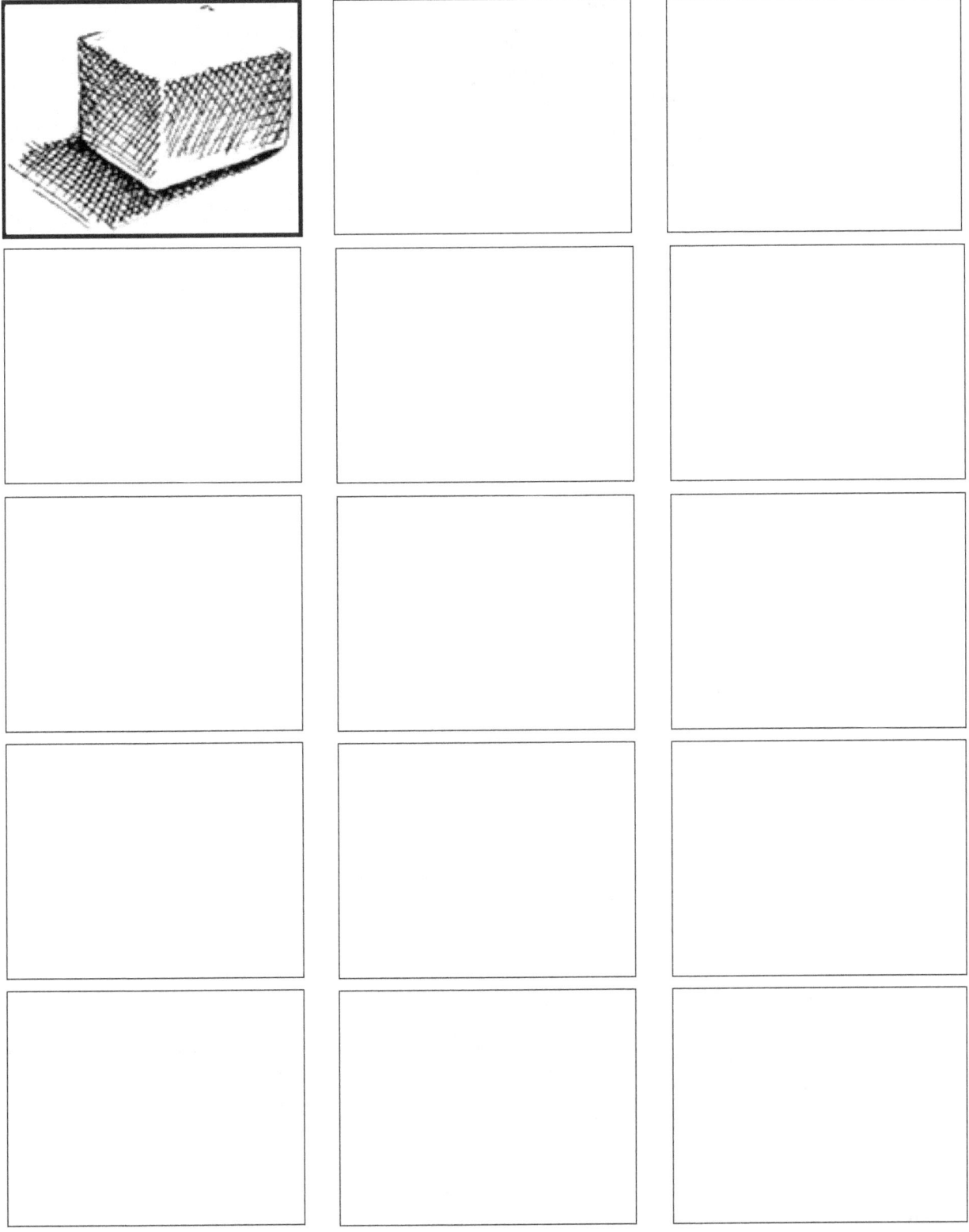

Draw cross hatch

(Use 4B, 6B and 8B Pencil)

Ex :- 21

Light to dark ⇒

(Move your pencil left to right direction)

Pg-21

Draw wave line   (Use 4B or 6B Pencil)

Ex :- 22

Draw wave line ⟹ (Move your pencil left to right direction)

Pg-22

Draw wave line

(Use 4B or 6B Pencil)

Ex :- 23

Draw wave line ⬅ (Move your pencil right to left direction)

Pg-23

Draw sea wave (Use 4B or 6B Pencil)

Ex :- 24

Draw sea wave ⇒ (Move your pencil left to right direction)

Pg-24

Draw an oval without compass or any object (Use 4B or 6B Pencil)

Ex :- 25

Draw oval

Draw circle without help of any object (Use 4B or 6B Pencil)

Ex :- 26

Draw circle

Pg-26

Practice and improve your hand & finger balance with eye accuracy

Ex :- 27

Shades

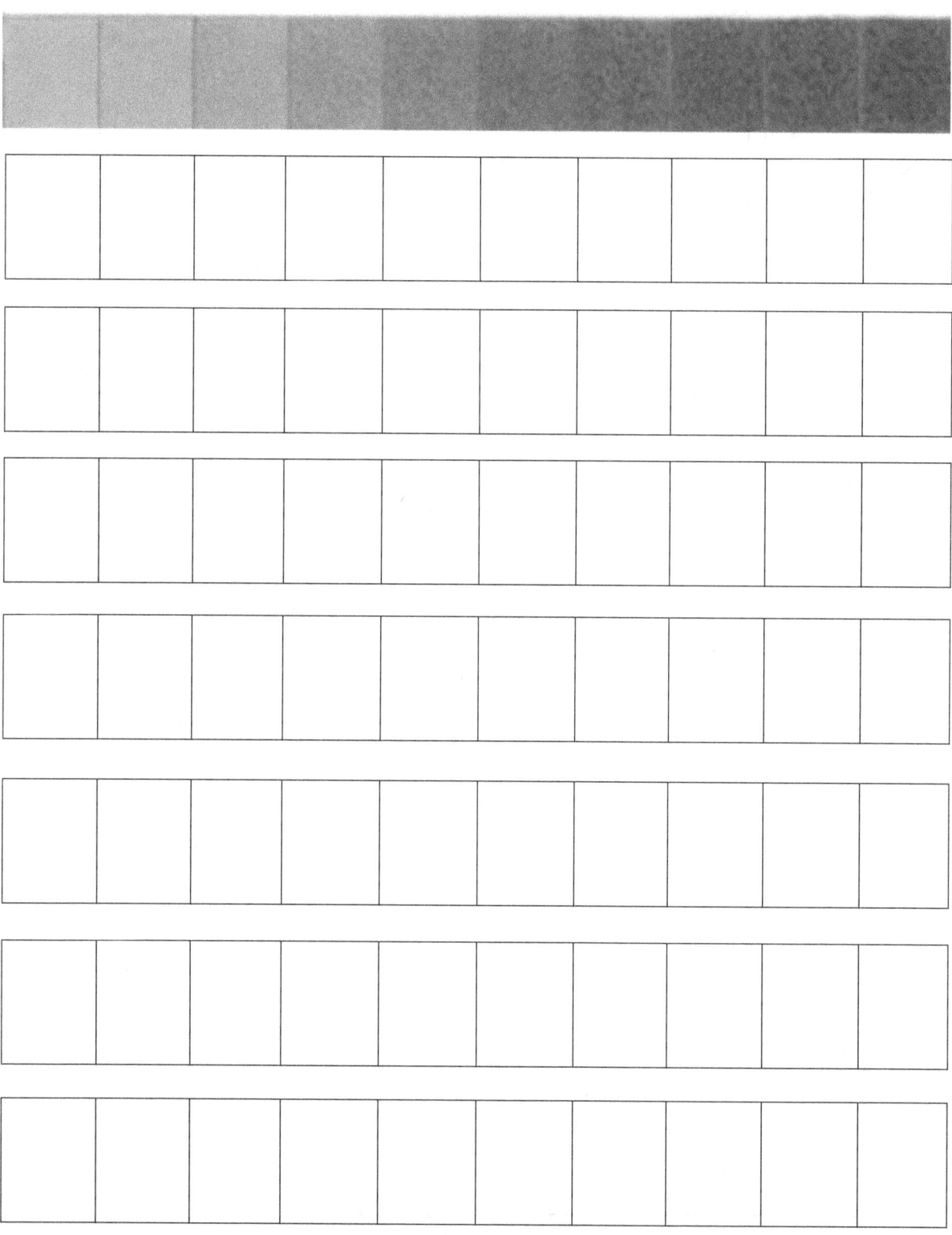

Pg-27

Accept the Challenge

Ex :- 28   Try to draw with Pencil Shading.

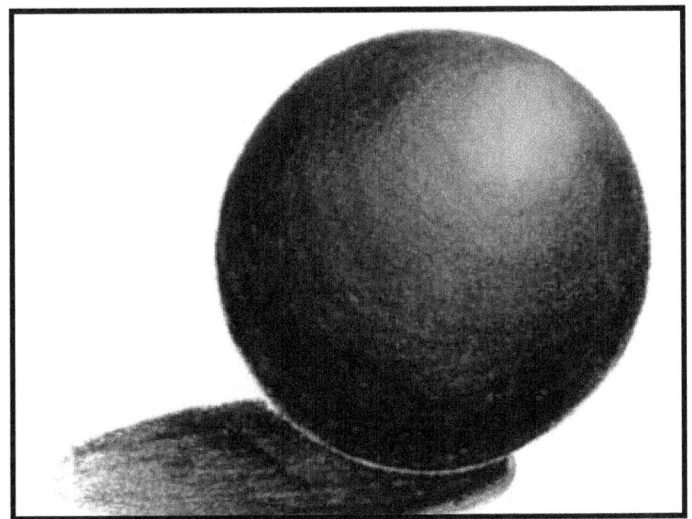

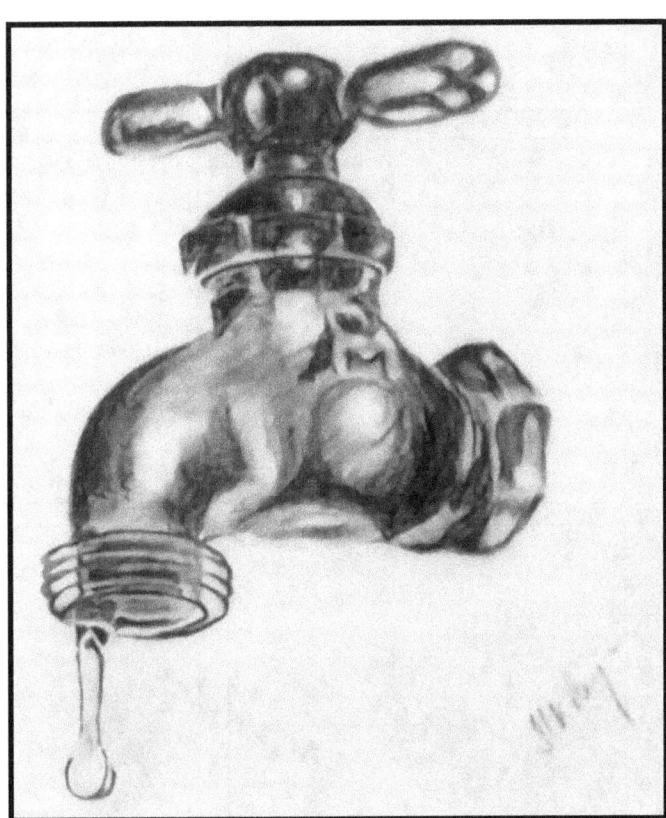

Practice and improve your hand & finger balance with eye accuracy

Ex :- 29   **Join the dots**

Join the dots in different angle, after that slowly increase the length between two dots and again join the dots.

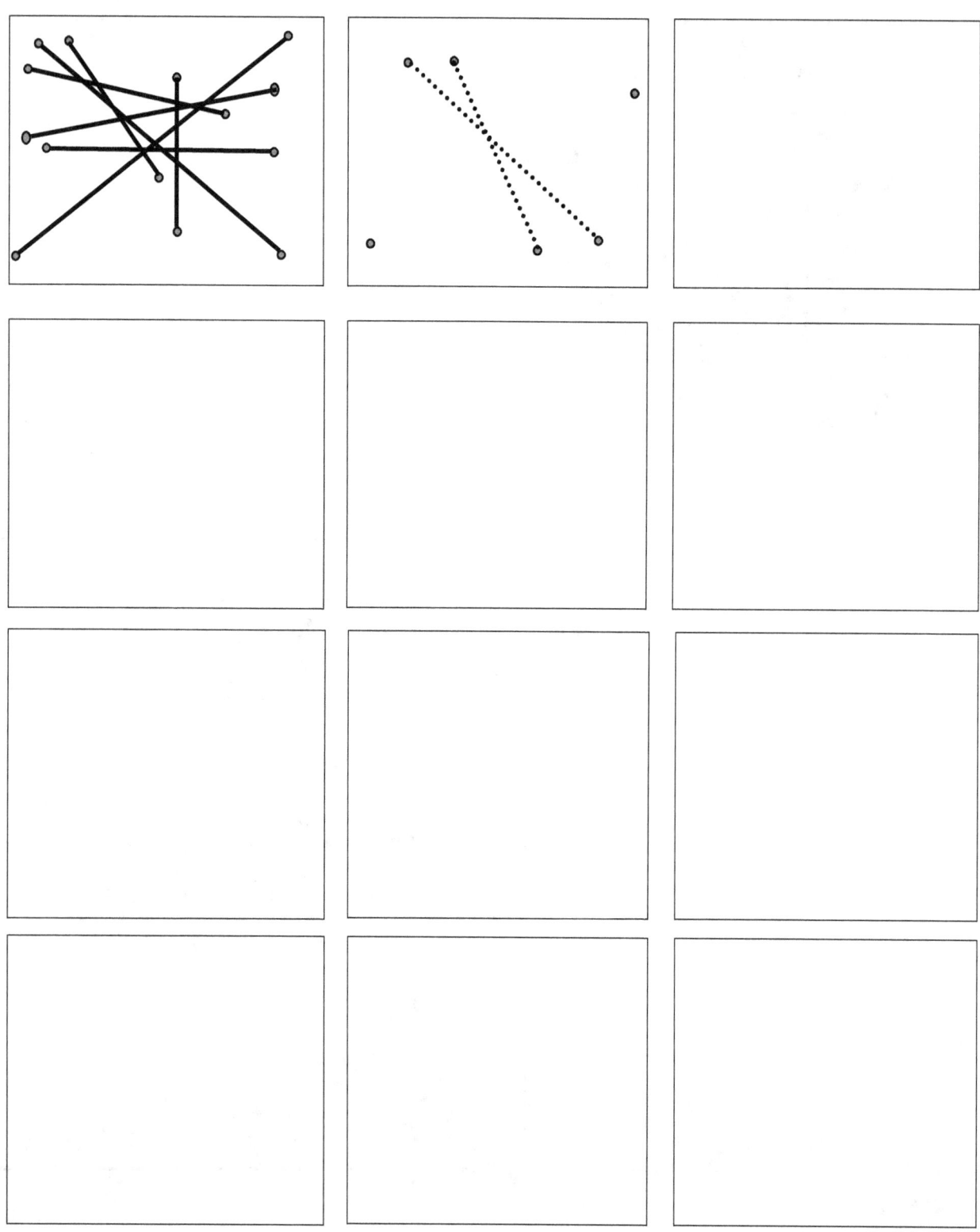

Pg-29

Practice and improve your hand & finger balance with eye accuracy

Ex :- 30 **Find the center position of line**

Join the dots in different angle, after that slowly increase the length between two dots and find the center position.

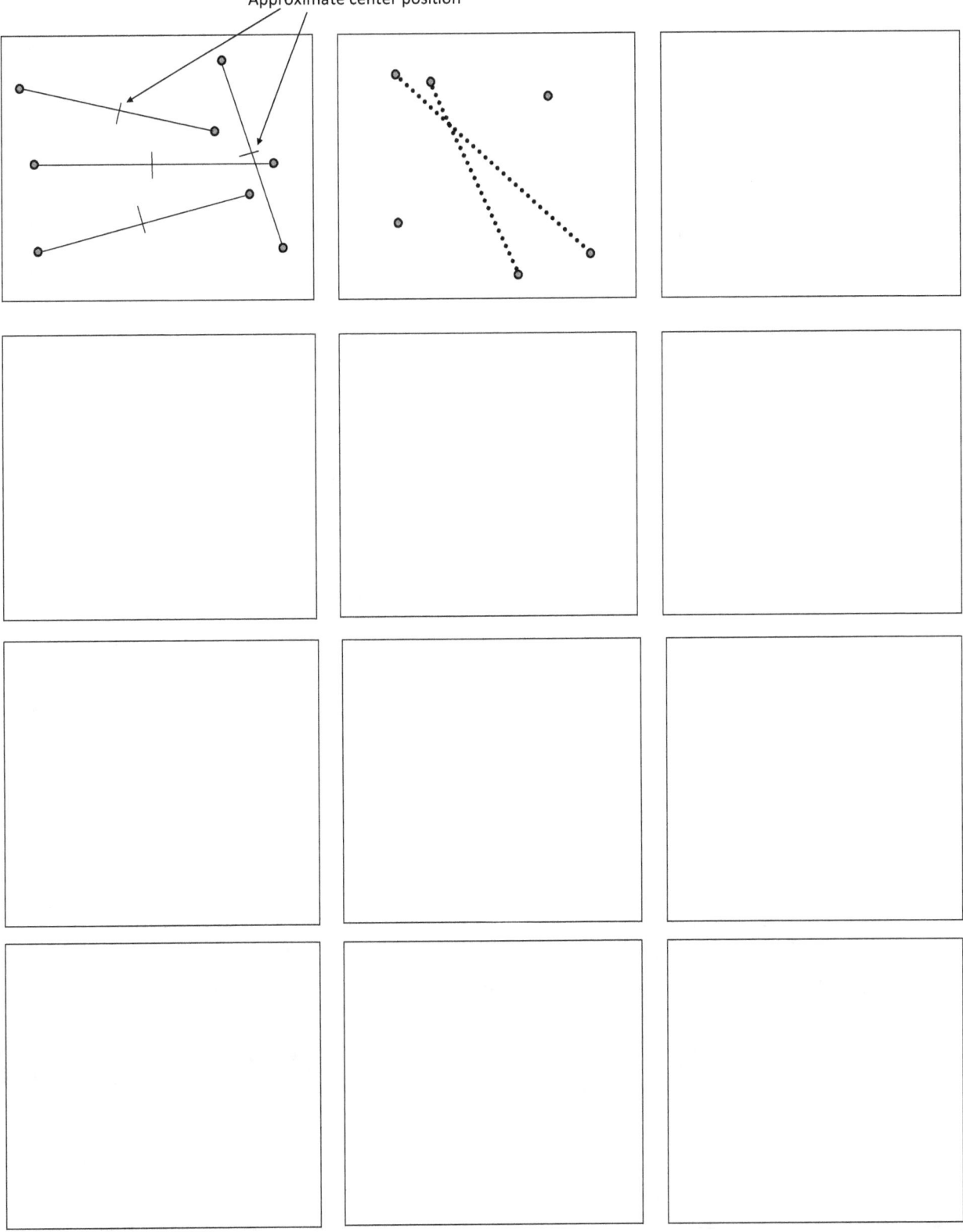

Pg-30

Practice and improve your hand & finger balance with eye accuracy

Ex :- 31 **Draw the double length line/Make a line with a twofold length.**

Join the dots in different angle, after that slowly increase the length between two dots and find the center position.

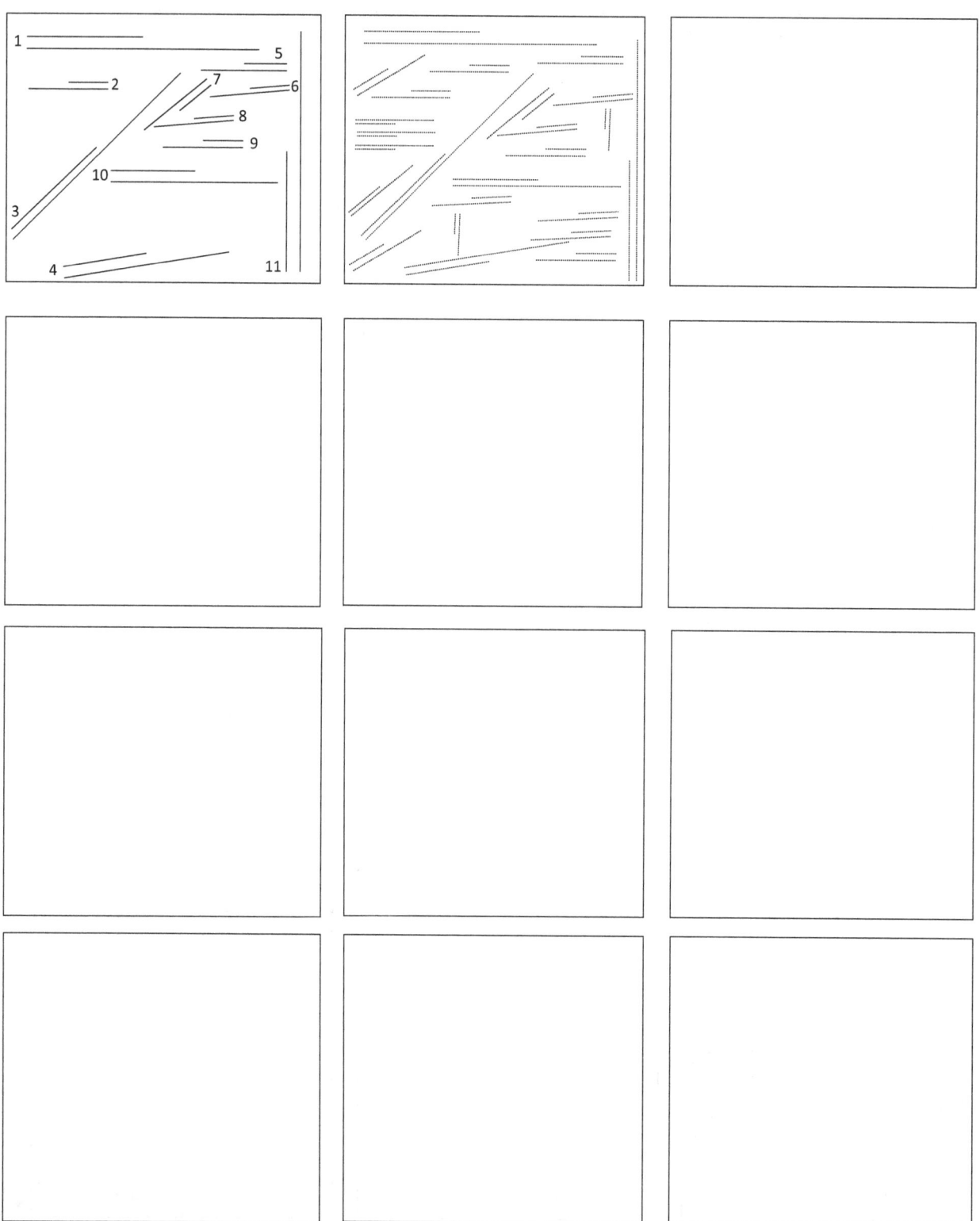

Pg-31

Practice and improve your hand & finger balance with Pressure Control

Ex :- 32 **Hatch (Light to dark)**

(Move your pencil Left to Right up direction)

Light   Medium: strokes have little more pressure   Dark: increase more pressure

Pg-32

Practice and improve your hand & finger balance with eye accuracy

Ex :- 33 **Cross Hatch**

Pg-33

Practice and improve your eye, hand & finger coordination

Ex :- 34 **Cross Hatch layer by layer**

- Wider gapes between lines = Light tone
- Narrow gapes between lines = Dark tone

It is a technique of shading which creates darker shades. It uses layers of **hatching**, Placed at drawing lines from different angles. Narrow gapes to wider and create impression of dark to light, opposite light to dark.

| Hatch | Cross Hatch | Three Layers | Four Layers | Light to dark gradation |

I hope you enjoyed the practice. These exercises are more powerful than they may seem. ***But don't*** limit your practice to just these exercises. Let your imagination go wild and invent your own warm-ups and challenges.

Sketching Challenge

Ex :- 35 Try to draw with Cross Hatching

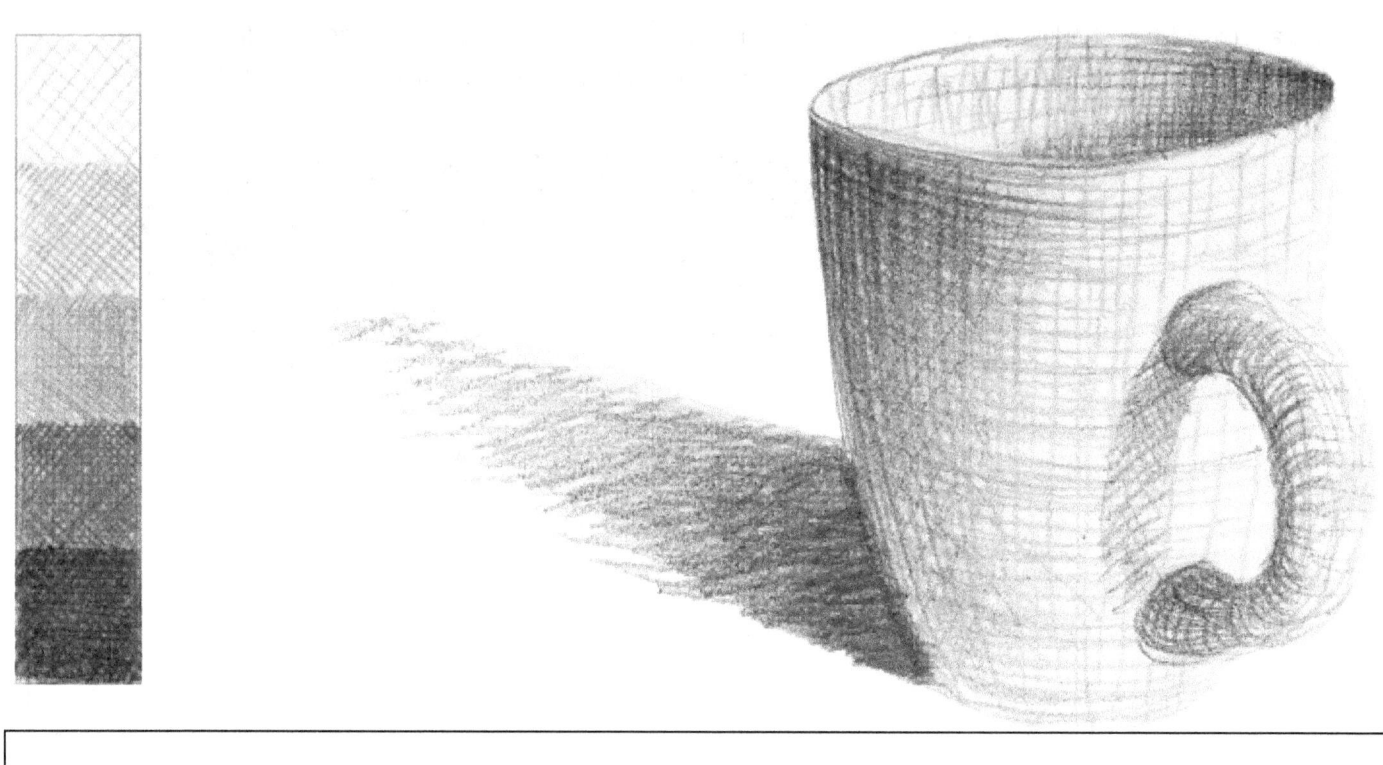

Pg-35

Sketching Challenge

Ex :- 36 Try to draw with Cross Hatching

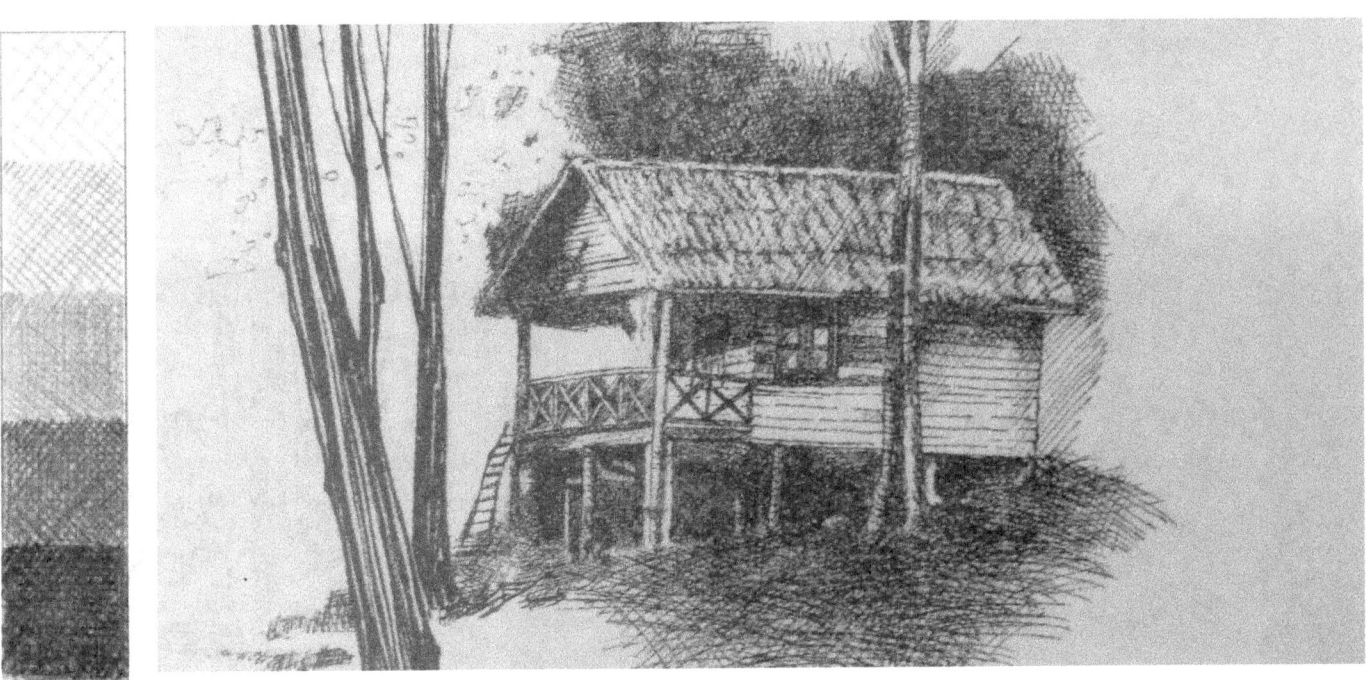

Sketching Challenge

Ex :- 37   Try to draw with Cross Hatching

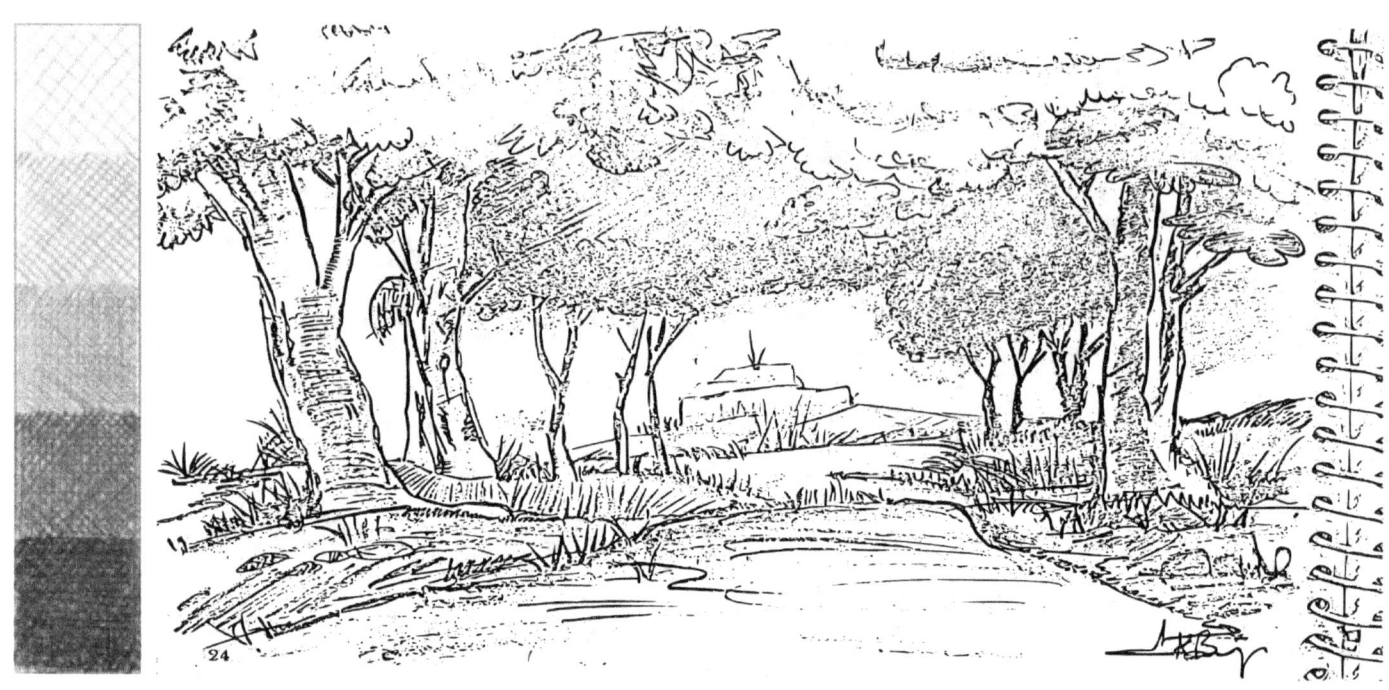

Sketching Challenge

Draw a picture of any object around you using your imagination.

Sketching Challenge

Draw a picture of any object around you using your imagination.

Sketching Challenge

Draw a picture of any object around you using your imagination.

Sketching Challenge

Draw a picture of any object around you using your imagination.

Sketching Challenge

Draw a picture of any object around you using your imagination.

Sketching Challenge

Draw a picture of any object around you using your imagination.

Sketching Challenge

Draw a picture of any object around you using your imagination.

Sketching Challenge

Draw a picture of any object around you using your imagination.

Sketching Challenge

Draw a picture of any object around you using your imagination.

Sketching Challenge

Draw a picture of any object around you using your imagination.

Sketching Challenge

Draw a picture of any object around you using your imagination.

Sketching Challenge

Draw a picture of any object around you using your imagination.

Sketching Challenge

Draw a picture of any object around you using your imagination.

Sketching Challenge

Draw a picture of any object around you using your imagination.

Sketching Challenge

Draw a picture of any object around you using your imagination.

Sketching Challenge

Draw a picture of any object around you using your imagination.

Sketching Challenge

Draw a picture of any object around you using your imagination.

Sketching Challenge

Draw a picture of any object around you using your imagination.

Sketching Challenge

Draw a picture of any object around you using your imagination.

Sketching Challenge

Draw a picture of any object around you using your imagination.

Sketching Challenge

Draw a picture of any object around you using your imagination.

Sketching Challenge
Draw a picture of any object around you using your imagination.

Sketching Challenge

Draw a picture of any object around you using your imagination.

Sketching Challenge

Draw a picture of any object around you using your imagination.

Sketching Challenge

Draw a picture of any object around you using your imagination.

Sketching Challenge

Draw a picture of any object around you using your imagination.

Sketching Challenge

Draw a picture of any object around you using your imagination.

Sketching Challenge
Draw a picture of any object around you using your imagination.

Sketching Challenge

Draw a picture of any object around you using your imagination.

Sketching Challenge

Draw a picture of any object around you using your imagination.

Sketching Challenge

Draw a picture of any object around you using your imagination.

Sketching Challenge

Draw a picture of any object around you using your imagination.